An Aviator's Field Guide to
Tailwheel
Flying

An Aviator's Field Guide to
Tailwheel
Flying
Practical skills and tips for flying
a taildragger

Jason Blair

Aviation Supplies & Academics, Inc.
Newcastle, Washington

An Aviator's Field Guide to Tailwheel Flying:
Practical skills and tips for flying a taildragger
by Jason Blair

Aviation Supplies & Academics, Inc.
7005 132nd Place SE
Newcastle, Washington 98059-3153
asa@asa2fly.com | www.asa2fly.com

See ASA's website at www.asa2fly.com/reader/taildrag for the "Reader Resources" page containing additional information and updates relating to this book.

None of the material in this book supersedes any operational documents or procedures issued by the Federal Aviation Administration or other governing agency, manufacturers, schools, or operator standard operating procedures.

ASA-TAILDRAG
ISBN 978-1-61954-589-2

Printed in the United States of America.
2022   2021   2020   2019   2018   9 8 7 6 5 4 3 2

Cover photo: Aimee Heckman

Library of Congress Cataloging-in-Publication Data
Names: Blair, Jason, author.
Title: An aviator's field guide to tailwheel flying : practical skills and tips for flying a taildragger / Jason Blair.
Description: Newcastle, Washington : Aviation Supplies & Academics, Inc., [2018] | Includes bibliographical references.
Identifiers: LCCN 2017056450| ISBN 9781619545892 (trade pbk. : alk. paper) | ISBN 1619545896 (trade pbk.)
Subjects: LCSH: Taildragger airplanes—Piloting. | Air-pilot guides.
Classification: LCC TL711.T28 B53 2017 | DDC 629.132/52—dc23
LC record available at https://lccn.loc.gov/2017056450

Contents

Acknowledgments

A special thanks to Greg Brown, Jonathan "JJ" Greenway, and Kevin Spaulding for their help in reviewing the content of this book. Their guidance and input were extremely valuable throughout the writing and finalization process.

Thanks very much to all of these individuals for the years of friendship and their help on this project.

Introduction

Flying a tailwheel aircraft is oftentimes thought of as being "more difficult" than flying a tricycle-gear aircraft. In reality, it is not necessarily harder, but takeoffs and landings in tailwheel aircraft might best be described as being flown "differently." Most of the fundamentals that are learned in tricycle gear flying are exactly the same as those used when flying a tailwheel aircraft.

Since the Federal Aviation Administration (FAA) does require that specific training and an endorsement be completed in order to qualify to pilot tailwheel-equipped aircraft, it seems obvious that notable differences must exist between these and tricycle-gear aircraft. This is exactly the truth, but it by no means indicates that the average pilot should be considered incapable of making a good transition to being a competent and proficient tailwheel pilot.

While some will contend that tailwheel aircraft are only older, antiquated things that modern pilots no longer fly, there is a next generation of tailwheels, and pilots must still learn how to fly these special aircraft. Many experimental aircraft, and a few new-production aircraft, are equipped with tailwheels and are not just flown by the last generation of pilots. With the next generation of pilots, these aircraft—both old ones that we still maintain and new ones being built by individuals or companies—have a place in our aviation community. Some tailwheel aircraft have performance characteristics that cannot be served by similarly sized tricycle-gear aircraft. With that in mind, I offer this book as a resource for tailwheel pilots in their transition and proficiency development process.

The intent of this book is not to teach you everything you need to know about tailwheel aircraft so you will have the ability to jump into the pilot's seat without further instruction and guidance from a competent instructor. No mere text could ever do that. It is intended to provide introductions, concepts, discussions, knowledge, and procedures that you can consider and incorporate into the training process to supplement the effort. Any good pilot will be well-served to learn as much as they can both during and outside of the actual flight training they receive. I am hopeful that this text will help facilitate that process!

I am not going to tell you that I have flown every tailwheel aircraft out there or that I am absolutely the most accomplished tailwheel instructor you can find anywhere. But as a competent instructor with many years teaching flight in tailwheel aircraft, I have learned a great deal that I can pass along to help you. Most importantly, I have learned that not every tailwheel aircraft is the same and not just any tailwheel-qualified instructor is the best choice for every tailwheel aircraft a pilot may choose to fly.

As you read this, you may think of additional things that could be covered. I certainly welcome any feedback and contributions readers have as we consider expansion of the material and improvement for future editions.

Chapter 1

Finding the Right Tailwheel Instructor

Before we dive into the details of what you will personally do as a tailwheel pilot, with my experience as both an instructor and examiner, I believe it is important to start with a discussion of how to find the correct tailwheel instructor. The "right" instructor does not just mean one who is tailwheel endorsed or even one who has flown the particular make and model of aircraft you will use in the training.

As you consider potential tailwheel instructors, key questions to ask include whether they have ever flown the particular make and model before, if they have flown tailwheel aircraft recently, and if they have previously taught someone in a tailwheel. Many instructors have flown tailwheel aircraft, but not all have taught someone in a tailwheel or conducted a tailwheel transition for a customer. Flying a plane yourself is different than instructing and training another person and ensuring they develop the competent knowledge, skills, and risk management to safely operate the aircraft.

Don't be afraid to travel if you don't find the right tailwheel instructor near where you live. This can even mean travelling with your plane if you have purchased a tailwheel plane. Another option if you already have an aircraft is to pay for a great tailwheel instructor to travel to provide training to you at your home airport. For most pilots, a tailwheel transition will not take weeks or months; with quality training and a little dedicated time, it can usually be satisfactorily completed (with a little cooperative weather) in a few days. This can keep travel expenses to a minimum while perhaps allowing a pilot to secure better training than might be available locally. This investment can be well worth the money, increasing the quality of instruction and potentially resulting in a tailwheel endorsement in an aircraft that is more similar to the one the pilot plans to fly.

When choosing an instructor, it is therefore important to also consider what type of aircraft you plan to fly after completing your endorsement. If you are shopping for a Citabria, getting your tailwheel endorsement with a local instructor who rents out their Cessna 170 for instruction may be fun, but travelling to another instructor who has a Citabria will probably be a better long-term training strategy. Shop around and be willing to travel to obtain the best instruction for your long-term training needs.

It is also important to consider insurance requirements. Many insurance underwriters will require a pilot to have specific experience in make and model of aircraft to be able to solo a tailwheel aircraft and for coverage to be in effect. The same holds true of an instructor who will provide training. This could be a factor in what type of aircraft you seek for your training and how much training you should plan to complete. It can also be a factor in choosing an instructor if you are looking for an instructor for an aircraft you own. Make sure the instructor has the required experience necessary for any insurance coverage to be effective (although hopefully you will never need it).

Although many people may automatically assume it's the case, it is always worth confirming that the instructor conducting your training has the proper commercial training to meet insurance minimums for the aircraft being flown. And once your training is completed, you will likely have to meet experience minimums to rent such an aircraft alone. The same will hold true if you provide your own aircraft both for you to fly as the pilot and to be used by the instructor. Insurance policies may also require that instructors provide a pilot history form detailing their experience in general, in tailwheel, and in particular make and model aircraft if the insurance policy does not have an open pilot warranty that offers a blanket provision for others to fly the aircraft with experience minimums.

Determine these questions prior to actually receiving instruction in the aircraft to ensure that if any unexpected damage happens during the training process, the insurance coverage in place will be effective. This discussion can be a major factor in choosing which instructor is appropriate to engage for your training.

So, with these considerations in mind, let's dig into more detail about tailwheel flying.

Chapter 2

The Basics

I would be lying if I didn't admit what the accident records indicate: Tailwheel pilots encounter more accidents, incidents, or—in most cases—minor mishaps with their aircraft than tricycle gear pilots. This is part of the reason that tricycle-gear aircraft are produced in larger quantities than tailwheel aircraft. Tricycle-gear aircraft are more forgiving of actions during takeoff and landing procedures than tailwheel aircraft, so it could be said that a tailwheel pilot must focus on the fundamentals and perform duties as the pilot-in-command with fewer breaks in attention than a tricycle gear pilot.

Flying a tailwheel aircraft requires a greater attention to detail, and that detail must be adhered to for a longer period of time, than flying a tricycle-gear aircraft.

We know that once a tricycle-gear aircraft is on the ground, its natural tendency is to continue to travel forward based on the position of its center of gravity in relation to the position of its gear. Even after landing, a tailwheel pilot must pay greater attention to rudder and brake control, because if the center of gravity is displaced, the tailwheel aircraft is more likely to turn about its center of gravity than a tricycle-gear aircraft.

As many old timers will remind a young tailwheel pilot, "keep flying it until you have it tied down."

Once a tailwheel aircraft is airborne, it is fundamentally the same as any other aircraft. This is why the majority of tailwheel transition training focuses on the takeoff and landing procedures. The main difference between tailwheel and tricycle-gear aircraft is the position of the center of gravity. In a tricycle-gear aircraft, the center of gravity is in front of the main wheels. But with the center of gravity *behind* the main wheels in a tailwheel, the airplane does not naturally tend to "pull" itself straight, a fact which allows the center of gravity to be more easily disrupted and may result in the tail spinning around the main gear. This is predominantly counteracted with right rudder.

For pilots who originally learn in a tailwheel aircraft, they may wonder what the big difficulty is of a tailwheel aircraft for people who transition into them. It is simply based on proficiency and experience. There is no reason that anyone should be afraid to learn to fly a tailwheel aircraft, but they should be aware that they will need to adapt to slightly different techniques and modify their style of flying to match the particular type of aircraft that they are flying. For a pilot with quality training and who makes a continued effort to maintain proficiency, tailwheel aircraft are equally—and in some cases more—capable and safe aircraft to operate.

One area in which tailwheel aircraft are certainly different than tricycle-gear aircraft is operations in crosswinds. A good tailwheel pilot will respect both the aircraft limits and—potentially more limiting—their own experience limits in tailwheel-equipped aircraft. ***It is not true that a good tailwheel pilot can operate in any wind that a tricycle gear pilot can operate in.*** The fundamental reason why a tailwheel aircraft cannot be flown in winds as strong as a tricycle-gear aircraft can is related to the aircraft's angle of attack while sitting on the ground. A tailwheel's three-point attitude without a nose wheel on the ground, having a tail wheel on the ground instead, allows crosswinds experienced on the tail and empennage surfaces to more easily dislodge the aircraft from a straight travel path down the runway. This results in the aircraft being more prone to yaw in a way that a tricycle-gear aircraft is less susceptible to experiencing. This can potentially result in a dreaded ground loop.

What exactly is the dreaded ground loop? We will talk more specifically about it later, but for the purposes of a basic understanding, it is a loss of directional control in the lateral direction that causes the aircraft to spin around, commonly resulting in a wing strike against the ground or other objects. A simple way to visualize a ground loop is that it occurs when the tail stops following the nose of the plane and instead spins around it. Obviously, you should try to avoid ground loops, but hopefully this description provides you with a simple mental image of what a ground loop is if the concept is new to you. In a later chapter, I will cover ground loops in more detail, including how to avoid them and how to respond if one occurs.

In a tailwheel aircraft, the pilot must cancel all sideways motion with respect to the ground at the moment of touch down. The longitudinal axis of the aircraft must be aligned with the centerline of the runway. The difficulty in this procedure is canceling the sideways drift with crosswinds and in gusty conditions. Most tricycle gear pilots spend less effort working to eliminate side-load and thus develop bad habits that make it more difficult to fly the tailwheel. These bad habits of tricycle gear pilots who infrequently fly tailwheels are some of the most common factors that cause problems when flying tailwheel-equipped aircraft.

A tailwheel aircraft is much more sensitive to pilot error than the tricycle. However, differences between various tailwheel aircraft make some more difficult than others, and some more forgiving of errors. Factors such as wheelbase length, overall length of the aircraft, height of the gear, type of struts, and many others can determine which aircraft are easier or harder to fly for a transitioning pilot. When you are considering your tailwheel training, find a good instructor who is familiar with the particular make and model, and spend the required time to really develop proficiency before heading off down the next runway in a 15-knot crosswind on your own or with family and friends.

Tailwheel aircraft do not have to be less safe to fly than tricycle-gear aircraft, but a strong understanding of the physics behind the configuration is needed to mitigate the problems that many have experienced when flying them. This must include an understanding of the dynamics of aircraft stability, rudder and brake control, and how the pilot can recognize a developing situation and react to it appropriately.

With this in mind, the next two chapters cover the first steps for a pilot operating a tailwheel aircraft: starting and taxiing.

Chapter 3

Getting It Started

I know you are probably wondering why I am beginning with something as simple as "starting" the aircraft, but in older aircraft it may be different than what you are familiar with doing.

Most modern tailwheel aircraft and many legacy aircraft have electric starters or have been upgraded to include them, but if you fly older tailwheel-equipped aircraft, they may not have electric systems and may require "hand-propping" to get them started. Hand-propping is something that many pilots have never experienced or been required to perform, and you should consider strongly whether or not you would be comfortable with this procedure (after training, of course). There is nothing wrong with saying it isn't something that you want to do!

Hand-propping an aircraft involves obvious safety risks, and a thorough understanding of how to do it properly is strongly recommended for anyone planning to conduct a hand-propping start of an aircraft.

You may even be thinking, "But if I have an electric system, I won't have to do this, right?" Well, not always. Some older aircraft have small batteries, and in colder conditions these batteries can become weak and not provide sufficient power to start the aircraft, requiring a hand-prop start of even an electrically equipped aircraft.

I humbly share a personal experience of just such a situation. I was once flying a Champ across the country and found myself in Utah on a very cold but completely clear day, and I wanted to get moving. But my battery, after sitting out in the cold for three days, was dead, and the engine was cold. So I found myself alone at 6:30 a.m. with what I perceived to be the only option—hand-propping the aircraft by myself.

Luckily, when the aircraft started, the two main wheel chocks held it in place, but since I had not chocked the tail wheel, the aircraft began to rotate. Also fortunately, it turned slowly. I managed to stop the turning and hop in, but not before about six other people had arrived at the airport to witness the event.

It was a lucky moment. The aircraft had been parked between two brand-new Mooney aircraft awaiting delivery by a dealer. The turn my aircraft made was such that it didn't run into these others, and I learned a valuable lesson. And I don't think I have ever returned to that airport.

It is generally a bad idea to hand-prop an aircraft when you are alone, but this doesn't mean it can't be done, either. The best procedures include having a competent person in the aircraft holding the brakes and ready to reduce power or lean the mixture if the starting is not going as desired. (This person can be a well-briefed and competent passenger, in some cases.)

As a side note, if the engine is cold, preheating is almost a necessity for any hand-propping. We get a little spoiled in our electrically powered starter aircraft in that we can crank and crank until the engine catches, even if it is cold. Think of how many times you would have to "throw" the propeller by hand to equal the same number of cranks when using an electric starter. I know I have become very tired trying this on a few occasions when the engine was cold.

If it is just about a dead battery, then strongly consider just charging it before you decide to start the aircraft by hand.

But in many aircraft like older Cubs, Luscombes, or Champs, an electrical system is not installed, and learning how to properly hand-prop these aircraft can open up an affordable class of aircraft for your flying!

If you are going to hand-prop an aircraft, spend some time learning more about techniques and safety. A good first step is to check out an AVweb article, "Hand-Propping Demystified," by Mike Hart. The book *Taming the Taildragger*, by John Ball, is a great resource for learning more about many of the important considerations. (You can find details about these on the Reader Resources webpage at www.asa2fly.com/reader/taildrag.) Also spend a little time surfing online videos to get a general idea of what hand-propping is all about, and then find a good instructor (or even an experienced pilot) who will properly teach you.

Chapter 4

Tailwheel Taxiing

Unless someone else pre-positions the aircraft for you on the runway, you will need to start the aircraft in its current location and then taxi it to the runway. This is a good thing, because taxiing also happens to be a great way to start to observe how a tailwheel aircraft "feels."

Taxiing in a tailwheel aircraft will initially feel different than it does in a tricycle-gear aircraft, but it can typically be mastered in a short period of time. What you will likely notice first is that the pilot's forward view is more limited than in a tricycle-gear aircraft, and depending on the type of tailwheel aircraft you are flying, the forward view may be completely blocked. In aircraft where forward visibility is more restricted, pilots can look further down the taxiway to keep taxiing in a straight line or may even choose to taxi using a side-to-side, tailwheel wiggle that allows them to look out the side windows as they work their way down a taxiway. This will make it look like the aircraft is taxiing in an elongated S pattern as it moves forward.

This restricted visibility while taxiing tailwheels must be considered when approaching other aircraft, as it may become impossible to see closely positioned aircraft or other obstacles. A large number of taxiing incidents have occurred in which tailwheel pilots who were unable to see directly in front of them collided with other aircraft or obstacles, and some of these incidents resulted in fatal injuries to the occupants and others on the ground. It never hurts to leave a little extra space in front of you, so consider giving more room between your aircraft and others if your visibility is restricted.

Taxiing a tailwheel requires a pilot to be more active in the rudder control during taxi. A combination of rudder deflection and, if equipped, tailwheel steering (commonly effected by springs to the tail wheel attached to the rudder controls)—takes longer to react to directional change inputs than the nose-steering systems on most tricycle-gear aircraft. Both tailwheel and tricycle-gear aircraft equipped with differential braking will experience similar control, but it is worth noting that a tailwheel aircraft will more easily experience a ground loop, even during taxi, if braking is not applied equally. Once disturbed from a straight taxi line, more effort will be required to bring it back to that position. Finally, as the pilot is making turns while taxiing, the tendency will be for the aircraft to continue the turn slightly after the rudder input has been neutralized, so "leading the exit of the turn" will help the pilot to realign the aircraft on a straight line after making a turn.

Most tailwheel pilots get in the habit of taxiing more slowly than tricycle-gear pilots. When starting the taxi, use only enough power to start the airplane moving, and then retard the throttle so the taxi speed equals that of a brisk walk. ***When taxiing, use brakes sparingly.*** Some tailwheel aircraft have limited brake utility due to older designs in the aircraft. You will find some with toe brakes and others with heel brakes. In a few classics, there may be no brakes. Use only what braking is necessary, do not apply the brakes abruptly, and do not make turns with a brake locked. With a little experience, you will learn to taxi and move the aircraft with little or no brake input.

As you taxi a tailwheel, the same control inputs on the stick/yoke will be applied as in a tricycle-gear aircraft. The mantra, "climb into the wind, descend away from the wind" is one way to remember where the stick/yoke position should be in consideration of the winds during the taxi. This means that if the aircraft has a headwind, the pilot will have the stick/yoke neutral or back, which keeps elevator up and tail down, and the aileron will be turned into the wind to keep the upwind wing down. For a tailwind (if it is stronger than propeller slipstream), the pilot will need to put the stick/yoke forward to keep the tail down and then turn the aileron away from the wind to keep the upwind wing from potentially elevating.

As pilots taxi, they should consider the position of the aircraft relative to the horizon. This position is the same position that the aircraft must be in when it contacts the ground for a three-point landing. How pilots taxi will be very similar to how they will fly the aircraft in this critical phase of flight, so close attention to good taxiing habits will lead to good flying habits in a tailwheel aircraft.

Good habits in flying tricycle-gear aircraft can be converted to good habits in a tailwheel aircraft. One of these is to properly apply aileron and elevator positions during taxi, during run-up, and while holding. The same corrections for headwinds, tailwinds, or quartering winds that apply in a tricycle-gear aircraft are made when operating a tailwheel aircraft, but it becomes a little more important to ensure they are being done. With the center of gravity rearward toward the tail, behind the main gear, ensuring these corrections are made mitigates any risk that the aircraft may rotate laterally or have the tail position increased (in the case of a strong headwind) to become closer to the takeoff angle of attack.

Chapter 5

High-Speed Taxiing

High-speed taxiing in a tailwheel aircraft is an operation that is risky and, in almost all situations, is an unnecessary risk for a pilot to take. You may have seen "the cool pilot" at the airport zipping by with their tail wheel off the ground as they taxi down to the departure end of the runway at 40 knots, but while they may think it looks cool, it is not normally a safe procedure to conduct. High-speed taxiing is in effect the beginning of a takeoff roll and then the prolonged abortion of the takeoff.

To complete a high-speed taxi, the pilot would use power to accelerate to an airspeed at which the tail can be lifted from the ground, and then taxi the aircraft on the main wheels in a level attitude. Direction would be controlled using rudders only. Abrupt brake use on a high-speed taxi will typically lead to a ground loop. Avoid high-speed taxi speeds in tailwheel aircraft.

This position is very susceptible to roughness in the taxi area, to pilot-induced oscillation, and to ground loop during the taxi. Although high-speed taxiing is an operation that should be avoided, I wanted to address it here since some pilots still use it and you may occasionally see it done.

Chapter 6

Normal and Soft-Field Takeoffs

You may remember back to your initial pilot certificate test when an examiner asked you to perform normal takeoffs and soft-field takeoffs. These two were each performed differently if you were flying a tricycle-gear aircraft. But in a tailwheel, normal and soft-field takeoffs will be performed virtually the same, which is why I lump the discussion about them together in this one section.

When a tailwheel aircraft is lined up on the runway before taking off, forward visibility may be somewhat obstructed by the nose high position, much like when taxiing. The amount that visibility is reduced will vary from model to model, but it will be a factor to some degree.

After lining up on the runway, the pilot will slowly apply appropriate power in a methodical and deliberate manner, being careful not to "cram the throttle forward." A normal takeoff usually includes application of full power over approximately a three-second count. Upon initial roll, the pilot will keep the stick (or yoke) neutral. As airspeed begins to register, the pilot will push forward on the stick until the aircraft balances on the main wheels with the tail off the ground. This is approximately the position of the aircraft when it is in level flight. Upon reaching sufficient airspeed for takeoff, slight back pressure will bring the aircraft into a climb, and the takeoff climb-out is initiated.

It is possible to "over push" forward on the controls, although this is not typically the most common problem pilots encounter when taking off. Many pilots are afraid of striking the propeller on the ground while the tail is raised during the takeoff run. While it is possible to do so, it takes a great deal of forward pressure and in most cases a substantial bounce in order for the nose to be in a position to cause a propeller ground strike. For many students, it can be helpful to sit in the aircraft and have an instructor (or multiple people, depending on the weight of the aircraft) lift the aircraft's tail to the point at which a propeller strike would occur, which will allow the student to visualize just how far forward the aircraft would need to be in order to actually strike the propeller.

A more common error a pilot may encounter is lack of compensation for the torque effects on the aircraft. When the tail wheel of the aircraft is lifted off the ground by the pilot pushing forward on the controls, the aircraft is more easily able to rotate to the left as a result of the standard left-turning tendencies that all aircraft encounter. Compared to a tricycle-gear aircraft, this is more pronounced in a tailwheel aircraft between the time that the tail wheel is lifted prior to rotation and when climb speed is reached. This means pilots may be more likely to encounter a tendency to veer left (for standard rotation engines) compared to what they are used to, and this could potentially result in a ground loop.

Pilots can learn to anticipate when the right rudder will be needed while the tail is lifted off of the ground. The application of the right rudder will mitigate the left-turning tendency experienced when the tail is lifted from the ground during the takeoff roll, keeping the aircraft travelling straight down the runway until the rotation off the ground is completed. Torque is more noticeable than in a tricycle-gear aircraft, since the three-point attitude during takeoff and the propeller rotation on the plane is not perpendicular to the plane of motion.

Takeoff procedure:

1. Line up the aircraft on the runway with the tail wheel straight.
2. Without coming to a complete stop, release brakes.
3. Apply power slowly (three-second count) with the stick back.

4. Raise the tail off the ground to an attitude that is roughly equivalent to a level flight attitude.
5. Upon reaching an appropriate rotation speed, apply slight back pressure to the stick and fly the aircraft off the ground, climbing at V_Y (V_X for a short-field takeoff).
6. Continue the climb to the desired altitude at V_Y (V_X for a short-field takeoff until any obstacle is cleared).

During takeoff, common errors that a pilot may encounter include skipping, yaw fluctuation, and a takeoff stall.

Skipping

Skipping occurs when the pilot accelerates to an appropriate airspeed and rotates, but then allows the aircraft to settle back to the ground, contacting the main gear.

As soon as the wheels leave the ground, the plane will rotate about the CG, which is located aft of the main wheels, and so the arm is relaxed. This leads to the plane tending to settle back down if back pressure is not maintained and slightly increased. This is more noticeable when there is an aft center of gravity in the plane (i.e., heavily loaded to the tail).

If skipping is encountered during takeoff, the pilot has two options: either increase the angle of attack to continue the climb, or decrease the angle of attack and keep the main wheels on the ground. Typically, the best practice will be to bring the nose slightly forward to allow airspeed to build, then rotate at a slightly higher airspeed and climb. This may mean bringing the aircraft back in contact with the runway and keeping pressure on the mains a bit longer to build the airspeed necessary for a clean takeoff. The reason this is typically the preferred method is that if the aircraft is settling back to the runway, it is an indication that not enough airspeed is present during the initial rotation to allow the climb to continue. A little pilot-in-command (PIC) judgment is required to make this evaluation, and in aircraft with greater power, it may be possible during some limited skipping to increase the angle of attack to continue the climb.

In either case, once the skipping has been minimized, the aircraft may once again be rotated off of the ground, and even gaining speed in ground effect (if sufficient runway is available) can allow enough airspeed to be gained to continue the takeoff.

If runway is limited, skipping becomes pronounced, or side loading is experienced, the best reaction is to retard the throttle to idle, abandon the takeoff, and flare into a three-point stance to in effect "land," stop, taxi back, and try it again.

Yaw Fluctuation

During takeoff, the plane will yaw slightly about the longitudinal axis. This can be corrected with rudder trim, if available, or rudder pressure. If there is a strong crosswind, this tendency will be pronounced, and for many tailwheel pilots the best practice is to turn the aircraft into the wind for the climb if no obstacle danger is present.

The most common error during takeoff occurs as the aircraft begins to yaw, and the pilot overcorrects with the rudder to counteract the yaw and ends up traveling in the opposite direction. This leads the pilot to overcorrect back in the opposite (original) direction, and the process begins to multiply. This condition can lead to a ground loop on takeoff, but can be corrected by simply inputting smaller rudder corrections to correct for the yaw fluctuation.

Takeoff Stall

Over-rotation during the takeoff can initiate a takeoff stall. This leads to a tail hook re-landing of the aircraft. This condition is avoided by simply not over-rotating. If over-rotation does occur, the pilot can respond by lowering the nose a bit to decrease the angle of attack and re-establish an appropriate climb attitude.

Chapter 7

Short-Field Takeoffs

In a tailwheel aircraft, the short-field takeoff is not very different from the normal takeoff. However, a few minor differences in making a short-field takeoff are important to note.

After applying full power to the aircraft during the takeoff roll, instead of raising the tail above the ground to a level flight position, the pilot will lift the tail only slightly above the ground. In most cases, this will mean the tail is approximately 6–12 inches off the ground.

As the aircraft rolls down the runway gaining airspeed, the pilot will maintain this tail position until the aircraft reaches V_X. Upon reaching V_X, the pilot will hold back pressure to the stick and climb the aircraft at V_X until all obstacles are cleared. After reaching a safe altitude, the pilot will then continue the climb to the desired altitude at V_Y.

During this procedure, the aircraft will be flown off the ground at a slower airspeed than during a normal takeoff and will be climbed at V_X instead of V_Y. This requires that the aircraft be taken off at an airspeed that is closer to stall than a normal takeoff, so the pilot should remain cautious during this type of takeoff.

Short-field takeoff procedure:

1. Line the aircraft up on the runway.
2. Release brakes.
3. Apply power slowly (three-second count) with the stick back.
4. Raise the tail slightly (approximately 6 inches) off the ground.

5. Allow the aircraft to fly itself off the ground in this attitude at V_X and continue the climb until all obstacles are cleared.
6. Continue the climb to the desired altitude at V_Y.

Many tailwheel aircraft have wonderful short-field takeoff characteristics, and for pilots who learn their aircraft well, this can open doors to a new set of airports and fields that they can visit with these capable aircraft.

Chapter 8

Tailwheel Aircraft Landings

Landings in a tailwheel aircraft are different animals than in a tricycle-gear aircraft. This is what scares transitioning pilots the most—tailwheel landings are the source of rumor, conjecture, and horror stories. But in reality, it is just a skill that a pilot must develop and become proficient in completing in order to fly tailwheel aircraft. It is not impossible, and with a good instructor, tailwheel aircraft landings can be fun to learn and serve as a new challenge to develop new pilot skills.

If I had to choose a single piece of advice to give you about tailwheel landings, it is to not overestimate your skills in the beginning or when transitioning between makes and models of aircraft.

Take it slow, and learn the plane. When you go out for the first time in an aircraft, don't do it in strong crosswinds, on short runways, or with the pressure of completing a trip or taking friends flying. Build these skills, and be willing to say "no" on some days. You can build up to more challenging conditions.

Most tailwheel operations use one of the following three basic types of landings:

- **Three-point landing**—All three wheels of the aircraft touch the ground at the same time, and backward stick pressure is continually applied as the aircraft settles to the ground and begins the rollout portion of the landing.
- **Wheel landing**—The two main wheels of the aircraft are allowed to touch the ground with the tailwheel elevated off

the ground through the runout on landing until the tail is no longer able to maintain lift.

- **Tail-low wheel landing**—The tail-low wheel landing is a combination of the two previous types of landings and is particularly useful for gusty conditions or strong crosswinds. In many cases, the upwind wheel and the tailwheel contact the runway at the same time, and then the downwind wheel contacts the ground as the aircraft slows down.

So why do we have different types of landings, and which one is better?

Well, none of the landings is necessarily better than the other. It can be argued that one or the other may be more applicable in certain situations, but it depends on the situation, the aircraft, and the pilot's proficiency. I will discuss the benefits of each below, but if you find someone chastising you because you did one or another, don't worry about it—choose the landing that you feel safest and most proficient at completing.

In general, threshold speed is more important in a tailwheel aircraft than it is in a tricycle-gear aircraft. This means that a normal approach is a powered approach. By maintaining a powered approach, positive control of the descent angle and the flight path is maintained. Along with this control, the engine is kept warm, which lessens the chance of carburetor icing; more elevator pressure is maintained, keeping the slipstream for flare alive so the airspeed can be lower; and less change in attitude for flare is necessary for the glide approach. The tailwheel aircraft is designed to land at the stalling speed angle of attack, so there must be enough elevator pressure at the minimum airspeed to still pitch the nose up at this point. The descent rate is then controlled not by the attitude, but the power in the approach.

In all tailwheel landings, no matter which type you are conducting, tracking the centerline of the runway is critical. To avoid an increased potential for a ground loop, or the momentum of the tail becoming displaced to the side behind the center of gravity, it's important to focus further down the runway and eliminate any side slip. The track of the aircraft must be aligned with the centerline of the runway.

If a minimal amount of side drift is experienced, a pilot may be able to correct using rudder, but at some point either the aircraft's capability or pilot skill will be exceeded, and a side drift during landing will not be recoverable.

One noticeable difference a pilot will discover in a tailwheel aircraft is the position of the nose and the visibility that the pilot has over the nose. In many aircraft, the visibility directly forward is limited due to the high nose position. For visibility on landings, many tailwheel pilots do not make straight approaches, but instead maintain a constant arc or an angular approach. This is more useful when performing three-point landings and is less necessary when performing a wheel landing, which affords the pilot a better view of the landing.

In one of my favorite aviation books, *The Cannibal Queen*, Stephen Coonts describes and discusses tailwheel landings:[1]

> The benefits of the three-point, full-stall landing—when the mains arrive on the deck, you want the tail wheel down simultaneously or as soon as thereafter as possible. Most tailwheels are steerable, so when coupled with the effect of the rudder, you can prevent the plane from weathercocking—if the tail wheel is on the ground and you are holding it down with full back stick. If it's up, all you have is rudder and you may not have enough.
>
> Some tail-wheel pilots feel more comfortable with wheel landings in gusty conditions. A wheel landing is flown at a slightly higher approach speed than a full-stall and the plane is literally flown onto the runway at that speed. The mains touch while the tail is still up in the flight attitude. The pilot lets the plane decelerate while working stick and rudder to hold the plane straight and overcome the effects of crosswind and gusts. If everything goes right these landings work out. Yet if something goes wrong, such as too much wind or a misapplication of the stick or rudder, the plane will be badly damaged in the resulting accident. Perhaps totally demolished.
>
> The amount of dynamic energy varies with the square of the speed, so obviously an accident at 35 mph will result in much less damage than one at 70 or 75. The old tail-wheel pros I have talked to recommended the full-stall landing, which is precisely why I use it exclusively.

1 Stephen Coonts, *The Cannibal Queen* (New York: Pocket Books, 1992), 274

Scrub off every knot you can before you put her on the ground, then if things go to hell, all you'll have to worry about is a scraped wingtip and damaged pride.

The Three-Point Landing

In most tailwheel aircraft, the three-point landing is the normal landing position. The approach for a three-point landing in a tailwheel is very much the same as it is in a tricycle-gear aircraft. As the aircraft nears the ground, the aircraft is flared to a three-point position with the nose slightly up. Then as the aircraft slows down, the pilot should make a serious attempt to keep the aircraft flying as long as possible and apply continual, slow back pressure to the stick. When the airplane finally stalls, it will settle to the ground in the three-point position, and the rollout is continued using the rudders for directional control.

During the rollout, the stick must be kept back in order to keep the angle of attack high enough to maintain a stalled position. The initial rollout is typically the most dangerous part of the landing for pilots transitioning from tricycle-gear aircraft to tailwheel aircraft, due to their lack of experience with having to fly the aircraft beyond the landing. Brakes should be applied only as necessary.

During the three-point landing, the key is to keep the stick coming back through the flare in a slow, constant motion to keep a stall condition for landing. This must be continued at the same rate as the aircraft settles to the ground, and after the aircraft is on the ground on all three wheels, the stick must be held full back to keep the aircraft's angle of attack in a fully stalled position and the aircraft firmly on the ground.

The goal is to get the tail wheel to touch at approximately the same time, or even just a couple inches before, the main wheels.

Primary Steps in a Three-Point Landing:

1. The pilot begins the approach at a normal airspeed and aligned with the runway.
2. When the aircraft nears the runway, the aircraft will be pitched slightly up into the three-point stance for the touchdown. As the pilot pitches the aircraft for this position,

and once the runway can be made, power is reduced smoothly for landing.

3. As the aircraft settles toward the ground, the pilot will continue to slowly add back pressure to the stick/yoke to keep the aircraft in the three-point stance through the point of touchdown, which should occur at stall speed in a full stall condition.

4. Once the aircraft has touched down on the ground on all three wheels, the pilot should apply full back pressure to the stick/yoke to keep the aircraft at an angle of attack that will not allow it to become airborne again; this will also provide for full steering with the tailwheel on the ground by adding pressure to the tail through the elevator position.

5. As the aircraft rolls out, the pilot will need to maintain diligent control of the rudders to keep the aircraft rolling straight down the runway.

6. The pilot will apply brakes as needed during the rollout to stop or taxi, but only after the aircraft is under control using the rudders.

Three-point landings are the first landings that most tailwheel students will encounter, and students should be proficient at these prior to attempting wheel landings. These are good, safe landings that allow the aircraft to contact the runway at the minimum controllable airspeed and provide quick stopping for soft and short fields.

The Wheel Landing

The ability to perform a wheel landing is one of the maneuvers that sets a tailwheel aircraft apart from a tricycle-gear aircraft. This maneuver has been described as having a variety of uses, and while some of these are accurate, some are highly inaccurate in their reasoning. While the standard landing for most tailwheel aircraft is a three-point landing, a wheel landing can offer advantages in some circumstances. The main advantages of the wheel landing include the following:

- It offers the maximum controllability of the airplane through the touchdown point.
- It provides reduced susceptibility to gusty wind conditions.
- Visibility is increased during the landing run.
- The speed at which the aircraft is touched down to the ground is controllable and well above the stall speed.
- It allows for easier transition between different models of aircraft.
- It is the most stable landing when an aircraft is overloaded or iced up, or for night landings when speed of touchdown is more critical.

A wheel landing occurs when the landing is made on the front main gear with near-level attitude without allowing the tail wheel to contact the ground upon initial landing. During this landing, the pilot will maintain a quicker airspeed. ***Precise control of vertical descent speed must be made to stop the aircraft from bouncing upon initial touch.*** The wheel landing will result in a longer landing run than a three-point landing due to the higher touchdown speed and the fact that the tail will be maintained in a raised position until all flying speed of the tail is lost and the tail falls naturally.

Primary Steps in a Wheel Landing:

1. The pilot begins the approach at a normal airspeed and aligned with the runway.
2. When the aircraft nears the runway, the pilot will pitch the aircraft to fly mostly level and use power reduction to establish a minimum descent rate down to the runway.
3. As the aircraft settles toward the ground, the pilot will continue to fly level with the runway, establishing a minimum descent rate and potentially adding a slight bit of power just before touchdown.
4. All drift must be eliminated, potentially establishing a slightly upwind wing-down position using opposite rudder to minimize drift.

5. Focusing down the runway, the pilot allows the wheels to contact the ground and may add a slight bit of forward pressure to "keep the main wheels on the runway" with positive pressure. For many pilots, it is easier to trim the aircraft to require some back pressure on the stick during the approach and flare so that when the aircraft touches the ground, all the pilot is required to do is release some of that back pressure instead of having to actually apply forward pressure to the stick.

6. As the aircraft rolls down the runway on the main wheels, power is slowly cut completely, and the aircraft is kept on the main wheels by continuing to apply forward pressure to the stick until the tail is no longer able to fly. This should end up being full forward stick pressure.

7. As airspeed decreases, the tail will lose adequate airflow to "keep flying," and the pilot can allow the tail to settle to the runway.

8. Once the tail is on the ground, full aft controls are input to keep the tail on the ground through the remainder of the rollout.

9. As the aircraft rolls out, the pilot will need to maintain diligent control of the rudders to keep the aircraft rolling straight down the runway.

10. The pilot applies brakes as needed during the rollout to stop or taxi, but only after the aircraft is under control using the rudders.

The essence of a wheel landing is to fly the aircraft onto the ground in a controlled manner. The aircraft is actually still flying while on the ground, and simply removing power after touchdown allows the aircraft to slow down and the tail to fall after lift has broken down.

If you are going to perform wheel landings, it is important to practice them regularly or continue to receive periodic oversight from an experienced tailwheel pilot or instructor. The reason that wheel landing practice is critical is that it allows a pilot to place the landing gear on the ground with a lower angle of attack and higher speed, hence with a greater degree of control.

Tail-Low Wheel Landing

The tail-low wheel landing is a combination of the three-point landing and the full wheel landing and is typically used during stronger winds and/or crosswind conditions. The tail-low wheel landing allows the pilot to maintain rudder control through the landing without exposing the aircraft to the full nose-level attitude of the wheel landing.

Steps in a Tail-Low Wheel Landing:

1. The pilot begins by starting the approach at a normal approach speed.
2. When the aircraft nears the ground, the pilot begins a flare to bring the aircraft to an attitude that will keep the tail from touching the ground during landing, typically aiming to keep the tail approximately 6 inches from the ground.
3. In the flare, the aircraft will be kept in this attitude, and the pilot must control the aircraft's vertical descent speed so that the main wheels of the aircraft contact the ground with a minimum amount of descent speed.
4. Upon contact with the ground, the pilot applies slight forward pressure to maintain the pressure on the main wheels and maintain their contact with the ground, but unlike in the full wheel landing, the aircraft is not kept in a level attitude.
5. As the aircraft rolls down the runway on the main wheels, power is cut completely and the aircraft is kept on the main wheels by continuing to apply forward pressure to the stick until the tail is no longer able to fly. This should end up being full forward stick pressure.
6. Once the tail is no longer able to fly, the tail will fall to the ground. After the tail has fallen, the pilot will apply full back stick pressure to keep the tail on the ground and will continue to control the aircraft with the rudders.

The tail-low wheel landing is regularly used for crosswind conditions. When this is the case, the upwind wing often is dipped to counteract the crosswind condition. As the aircraft is landed in this condition, the upwind main wheel and the tailwheel will contact the ground prior to the downwind main wheel while crosswind aileron correction is added through the landing as the aircraft loses its flying speed. This can be one of the trickiest combinations of technique and procedure for a tailwheel pilot. The combination of the wheel landing and the crosswind landing poses the greatest potential for ground looping and must be carefully undertaken, and pilots must know their own personal limits—as well as the limits of their aircraft—in these types of conditions.

Chapter 9

Short-Field and Soft-Field Landings

The shortest possible landing in most tailwheel aircraft is the three-point attitude landing. This is based on the slower approach speed and the controllable position on landing for braking action. This is also true of the soft-field landing.

In both of these types of landings, the object is to get the aircraft on the ground and slowed to a taxi in a quick manner. The way in which a pilot accomplishes this for either a short-field landing or soft-field landing will vary to some degree based on the requirements of the field itself.

Short-Field Landing

As in all aircraft, the short-field landing is typically performed in order to use as little runway as possible, and it may require the aircraft to clear an obstacle at the landing end of the runway. A higher approach path is used for a short-field landing compared to a normal approach. As a tailwheel aircraft nears the ground in a short-field landing, the pilot brings the pitch of the aircraft into a three-point stance and allows it to contact the ground at a minimum airspeed. The higher approach path is aimed at a touchdown point that will allow the pilot to remain clear of any obstacles while also providing sufficient space to conduct a rollout, slowed by the use of braking action, without over-running the available landing area.

While some instructors will tell you that a wheel landing allows for a shorter field landing, this really is not the case. In fact, a wheel landing will typically result in using more runway than a properly conducted three-point landing, because in a wheel landing, the aircraft is approaching and contacting the ground at a higher airspeed than in a fully stalled three-point landing. Many pilots may find it easier to perform a "spot" landing when conducting a wheel landing due to the controlled use of power to determine the touchdown point, but when I really need to make a short-field landing, my money is on the three-point. If I discover that I am going to touch down beyond my intended (or required) point of touchdown, then that is a good time to go around and try it again.

For short-field operations in aircraft that have limited forward visibility, pilots can use a modified wheel landing that transitions quickly to a three-point stance. This will allow the pilot to continue to the point of touchdown with improved visibility and then transition right to a three-point stance shortly after touchdown to slow the aircraft quickly and keep the tail on the ground.

Soft-Field Landing

Soft-field landings can be done in either a wheel landing or three-point position, each having some benefit. With either, the key is to control the vertical descent speed and contact the ground with minimal downward force.

When doing a wheel landing on a soft field, the pilot is more able to allow for increased power to keep the aircraft rolling during the touchdown. This also minimizes the number of wheels on the ground creating drag, allowing the pilot to settle the tail wheel at a desired point. The danger of wheel landings on soft fields is that when the field is excessively soft, the aircraft may experience a forward moment if the main wheels are slowed quickly due to field conditions. Wheel landings on soft fields are best used when the field is grass and not overly soft, or when you expect rough field conditions that could cause damage to a more fragile tail wheel during the touchdown. Soft-field, wheel landings are also essentially mandatory when landing a ski plane.

The three-point, soft-field landing requires that the pilot land in the three-point stance at a minimum airspeed, although the touchdown point and approach may or may not have to take into consideration obstacles or the length of the runout, as is important in the short-field landing. After the aircraft contacts the ground, to avoid the potential of getting stuck in the soft field, the pilot keeps the aircraft in motion until it is on sufficient ground where this is no longer a concern.

Landing Challenges

The short-field landing and soft-field landing are virtually identical to the normal landings that tailwheel pilots perform on a regular basis, with only slight modifications to consider the approach path needed, the stopping distance, or the need to keep the aircraft moving after touchdown. In both cases, the key will be to use a full-stall landing technique in the three-point landing stance to provide the aircraft with the least possible chance of bouncing and to contact the ground at the slowest possible controllable airspeed. This further allows the aircraft, once on the ground, to maintain the greatest controllability for runout and taxi.

Common landing difficulties encountered during any landing are the bounce and the balloon:

- **Bounce (under-rotation)**—This occurs when the pilot does not raise the nose sufficiently or quick enough for the flare to land. The bounce is a firm contact of the mains or the three points with the ground, and the momentum of the CG will cause an instantaneous increase in the angle of attack. This increase in the angle of attack will commonly result in a short return to flight, which can rapidly be followed by a secondary bounce caused by exceeding the angle of attack when the momentum dissipates and the aircraft does not have enough energy to fly. If this is allowed to happen, it can result in continued bounces or worse. The pilot should never allow the aircraft to bounce more than twice without conducting a go-around.
- **Balloon (over-rotation or float)**—The balloon results from too much nose up and a slight climb instead of flare. If one of these bounces occurs, the pilot should transition to a three-point landing or go around. A balloon situation may result in a "tail hook" landing in which the tail actually contacts the ground first and then the mains fall to the ground as the angle

of attack exceeds the aircraft's stalling characteristics. If this occurs, either maintain full back pressure to keep the mains on the ground and stop them from bouncing, or if possible, perform a full go-around.

Chapter 10

Tailwheel Crosswind Operations

In tailwheel aircraft, crosswinds are probably responsible for more incidents and accidents than any other condition. Crosswinds require much more of the pilot's attention in a tailwheel aircraft than in a tricycle-gear aircraft. The primary reason for the increased attention demands is that tailwheel aircraft have a stronger tendency to "weathervane" into the wind. This does not mean that a tailwheel aircraft is any harder to fly or that it is more dangerous, but it does mean that the pilot must learn the aircraft's limitations as well as fully understand their own pilot limitations based on experience and abilities in that aircraft. Some crosswinds that a pilot normally would fly in while using a tricycle-gear aircraft are simply not appropriate to fly in while using a tailwheel aircraft.

Crosswind Taxiing

In a tricycle-gear aircraft, taxiing in a crosswind is largely the same as in non-windy conditions, except for the yoke control that pilots are supposed to apply (even though many tricycle-gear aircraft pilots rarely bother to do so). However, in a tailwheel aircraft, the center of gravity positioning requires pilots to be more active with control input and rudder control during taxiing operations. This may even require some assistance from a brake to keep the aircraft traveling straight down the intended taxi surface. The weathervaning tendency of the aircraft, if left unchecked, will allow the wind to blow the tail surface downwind and turn the nose of the aircraft into the wind, unless the pilot applies correction using rudder and/or brakes. In strong winds, it may even become necessary to "drag a brake" on the downwind side of the aircraft to keep the aircraft turned that direction for straight taxiing. Taxiing in extreme conditions may require turns to be made in only one direction due to the lack of enough rudder or brake to turn the aircraft away from the wind. Because of the weathervaning tendencies of a tailwheel aircraft, turning upwind will be easier than turning downwind, as the latter will require a longer turn radius.

The aircraft type will determine the level of effectiveness that you can expect during crosswind taxiing operations. As a general rule, however, note that if you are unable to taxi effectively in a certain direction due to a crosswind, unless the runway travels in another direction, attempting takeoffs or landings in that same crosswind that made taxi difficult will make takeoffs and landings even more precarious.

Crosswind Takeoffs

The requirements for crosswind takeoffs in a tailwheel aircraft are not greatly different than those in a tricycle-gear aircraft. The pilot must be concerned with the wind positioning and strength in order to counteract the tendency for the upwind wing to be lifted, which could lead to a potential wing-over condition in strong winds. This is normally corrected by adding aileron toward the upwind side of the aircraft during the takeoff, and this is gradually released as the aircraft begins to fly off the runway. The primary difference compared to a tricycle-gear aircraft is that the tailwheel pilot will need to exhibit greater rudder activity, since the tail will be lifted off the ground during the takeoff roll, and this will increase the aircraft's tendency to weathervane. This is largely due to the fact that the aircraft is no longer grounded at three points and will much more easily pivot about the horizontal axis if allowed.

When taking off, keep the upwind wing dipped into the wind using the aileron. This will help to prevent wind from getting under the wing. Using the aileron will require that the pilot also introduce opposite rudder to maintain directional control in a straight line down the runway during takeoff. This condition is similar to the standard crosswind landing correction that most pilots are used to making in a tricycle-gear aircraft. Continue to control the aircraft using the rudder and aileron combination as the aircraft rolls down the runway. Upon liftoff, continue to control the aircraft with aileron and rudder corrections. If the crosswind is excessive, many pilots like to turn into the wind slightly during climb, if the airport environment allows it, so that they no longer have to adjust for crosswind corrections.

Crosswind Landings

Crosswind landings are where most incidents or accidents in a tailwheel aircraft occur. In many cases, tailwheel aircraft simply cannot fly in crosswind conditions as strong as the crosswind conditions that can be handled by the tricycle-gear aircraft most pilots are used to flying. When flying a tailwheel aircraft, it's important to consider experience in and knowledge of the aircraft you are flying when trying to determine if your abilities can match the severity and conditions of the crosswind you are facing.

During a crosswind landing, keep the upwind wing dipped slightly and correct with rudder to maintain directional stability down the runway during flare and rollout. *A crosswind landing is performed as a three-point landing unless the conditions are very gusty.* This allows the pilot to keep a wing down, approach at the slowest possible speed, and on contact have less airspeed that will need to be bled off before the aircraft is brought to a stop or into a slow taxi.

For gusty crosswind landings, a tail-low wheel landing is performed. The three-point landing is in essence performed as a "two-point" landing for a crosswind. This is the result because the aircraft has a wing low position for the landing, and the downwind wheel is raised to compensate for the wind. As the aircraft slows down and the wing runs out of flying speed, the second main wheel will fall and the pilot will need to continue to add crosswind controls during the rollout.

In both types of landings, it is crucial that a zero-sideslip or drift condition be maintained for and throughout touchdown during a crosswind. This is important if the pilot wants to avoid ground-looping the aircraft in a crosswind landing.

Another method is to use a crabbed landing and kick-out method. This is a much more complex timing maneuver and should not be attempted unless absolutely necessary or except by a highly experience tailwheel pilot. The pilot maintains a crab until the moment just before touchdown and then kicks the rudder in the direction necessary to point the aircraft directly down the runway.

For crosswind landings, a strong consideration should always be finding another airport that has a runway more directly aligned with the wind. Do not think you *have* to land at the airport you started at. It would be better to find yourself landing into a stiff wind at another airport and needing to find a ride home than to find yourself wishing you hadn't landed at your home airport in a stiff crosswind that resulted in damages to your airplane—or worse.

Crosswind landings are the time when most pilots have the greatest susceptibility to ground looping the aircraft. Rudder control is vitally important during these operations. If the pilot finds that the nose is starting to veer one direction or the other, at times a quick jab on a brake will help keep the aircraft headed straight; however, if the pilot is not able to maintain directional stability with the rudder down the runway, the crosswind that exists is probably too strong for the aircraft, and the pilot is subjecting the aircraft unnecessarily to a greater potential for a ground loop.

Chapter 11

The Ground Loop

Any discussion of tailwheel procedures and characteristics would be incomplete without talking about the ground loop. The ground loop is probably the most feared occurrence that pilots think can happen in a tailwheel aircraft. It is also what most frequently causes damage to tailwheel aircraft. But ground loops are not inevitable—it's possible for tailwheel pilots to avoid ground loops during their careers as long as they understand the limitations of their aircraft, their ability based on their piloting experience, and how to properly avoid letting the aircraft get into this situation.

A ground loop occurs when the tail of the aircraft loses directional stability and rotates about the horizontal axis of the aircraft. This results in the tail wanting to spin around the nose of the aircraft as it is disturbed from a straight line. When this happens, the momentum will carry the tail partway or potentially all the way around until the tail is where the aircraft nose was originally, if no correction is made.

In many cases, the momentum will cause a wing to dip and may cause a wing strike on the outside of the ground loop, leading to a cartwheeling effect in which the other wing strikes as well. As the ground loop happens, directional control is lost and the aircraft will frequently travel off the runway surface and be subjected to potential hazards that exist off the runway, such as lights, ditches, or unimproved surfaces. This no doubt can cause damage ranging from minor to very severe, and no pilot would choose to be in this situation.

To avoid ground looping an aircraft, the pilot must be able to maintain proper rudder control at all times, even through what most tricycle-gear pilots would consider a moderate or slow taxi. Tailwheel aircraft have the potential to ground loop to some extent at virtually any speed of travel—the speed simply controls how much momentum will be available when the aircraft ground loops. This momentum will determine how far or bad the ground loop will become if it is encountered. It is for this reason that pilots should taxi slowly, perform landings that allow for appropriate stopping, and get themselves to a controllable taxi speed as soon as possible after landing.

However, the pilot should also be cautious not to over-brake. If aircraft braking is not applied smoothly and one side is favored, the aircraft will have a tendency to veer toward the side on which more brake is being applied. Once the tail is disturbed from straight travel, it will take greater rudder and brake pressure on the opposite side to bring the aircraft back to straight. Note that overcorrection can lead to a fishtailing effect that will gradually worsen and lead to a position in which the pilot no longer has enough rudder or brake control to stop the developing ground loop.

In most aircraft, if a ground loop begins to develop, the pilot has a couple of available options depending on the position of the aircraft or how far the ground loop has progressed. If the ground loop is occurring upon touchdown or slightly after, the best option will be to apply full power, steer the aircraft with the rudders, and go around. *A safe go-around is always better than a bad landing.*

If the ground loop has developed further, the pilot is no longer able to directionally control the aircraft, or a go-around is not possible, the pilot should immediately retard the throttle to idle and control the aircraft to the best of their ability using rudders and brakes to bring the aircraft to a stop. While doing so, the pilot should keep the stick/yoke all the way back to keep the tail of the aircraft on the ground and the nose up. This will keep the angle of attack high to decrease the aircraft's potential for becoming airborne again and additionally will minimize the potential for a prop strike as the aircraft travels through the ground loop.

Chapter 12

Considering Differences Between Tailwheel Aircraft

Like in other types of aircraft, there are differences between makes and models of tailwheel aircraft that can affect the way they feel to a pilot. But these differences can be a larger factor when flying a tailwheel aircraft than in a tricycle-gear plane. A few common differences are worth discussing as you think about switching between different makes and models, or even specific tail numbered aircraft based on what is installed on the particular aircraft.

Different Types of Tail Wheels

Not all tailwheels are exactly the same. In fact, the differences specific to a particular tailwheel can be a significant factor in how the aircraft will perform on the ground.

Modern tailwheel aircraft tend to be more easily steerable than older models, at least within a certain set of degrees. Modern tailwheel aircraft are most commonly steerable within approximately 30 degrees left or right. This is accomplished by tailwheel springs attached to the rudder controls that allow the pilot to exert a degree of force on the tail wheel itself when it is on the ground, allowing the tail to be steered by the pilot left or right through coordination with the rudder. In most of these, when a set limit has been exceeded—for example, greater than 30 degrees of tail wheel deflection left or right—the tail wheel becomes free castering, allowing it to spin freely. If this happens during a takeoff or landing, it becomes more likely that the pilot will encounter a ground loop. But as long as the tail wheel has not exceeded the limit to become free castering, the pilot will have greater control over the direction of the tail through the coordination with the rudder pressure, unlike some of the older tailwheel styles. This still allows the pilot to move the aircraft effectively on the ground by allowing the tail wheel to become free castering when necessary, but also limits the likelihood of this happening during normal operations. These coupled tail wheels keep the tail wheel tracking straight ahead under most circumstances and are easier for most pilots to manage.

One thing to watch for, and something I have encountered on a few occasions, is a tail spring that happens to fall off. If a tail wheel has experienced shuddering or vibration, most commonly as a result of a rough runway surface, the tail springs can be shaken loose and fall off. If only one tail spring falls off, the tail wheel will be canted to one side when the next landing is conducted. When the pilot sets the tail down, this can create a sideways motion, which if not caught quickly can result in a ground loop. A good preflight inspection of the tail springs can help limit the chances of this happening.

Some aircraft still have fully free-castering tail wheels that are not coupled to rudders and do not help the pilot track the tail forward through coordination with the rudders. Free-castering, tailwheel-equipped aircraft tend to be a little more susceptible to ground loops, and these aircraft make pilots more actively manage their forward direction than when in aircraft that are coupled. A free-castering tail wheel can spin freely at any point. While these generally tend to track forward when in flight, it is worth being careful when setting the tail down to ensure that the tail wheel is tracking forward in order to avoid any side motion.

Although not very common, a few aircraft still have post tail wheels that do not spin at all. These help track forward easily, but tend to skip and skid if any side load is encountered. In addition, any side loading or tracking by the pilot during the landing can tend to result in damage to the tail wheel itself.

On even fewer and mostly much older aircraft, a tail skid may be present. These are not commonly used on aircraft operated from pavement runways, and most aircraft that had them originally have been converted to wheels, but tail skids do still exist on some historic aircraft. If you are going to fly an aircraft equipped with a tail skid, first spend some time working with someone who has experience with one before setting out to fly one on your own.

Narrow or Wide Gear, Long or Short Aircraft

Aircraft vary in their lengths (longer or shorter) and in their widths (wider or narrower)—and the same is true of the gear on aircraft. These factors can make a difference in how easy it is to keep an aircraft tracking straight during takeoff and landing.

Typically, the longer the distance from the front gear to the tailwheel, the more difficult it is to displace the aircraft from tracking straight to result in a ground loop. Also, the wider the gear, the harder it typically is to displace the aircraft from tracking straight into a ground loop. So it is easier to avoid ground looping in a long, wide-geared aircraft than in a short, narrow-geared aircraft. To think of it simply, an aircraft with a gear footprint that is triangular and short will be harder to keep tracking straight.

Although this explanation is a little simplistic, it is an important consideration if you are transitioning between different makes and models of tailwheel aircraft. It is absolutely true that the structure of the gear footprint for the aircraft will have an effect on how the aircraft flies for the pilot.

Toe or Heel Brakes

Most modern, tricycle-gear aircraft are equipped with toe brakes. A few older ones, such as the Piper Cherokee, initially only had a singular hand brake. But not all tailwheel aircraft are equipped with similar brakes, some are equipped with heel brakes, and a few still do not have brakes at all.

It is more important to learn a bit about the brakes and their tendencies on tailwheel aircraft you will be flying than it is for tricycle-gear aircraft.

For pilots who have never flown heel brakes, they will need to learn to keep their feet in a slightly different position than they have used in other aircraft. A heel brake is most commonly flown either with the feet up resting on a rudder peg or with the feet at a slight angle, the heels to the side of the brake pedals, and the feet on the rudder peg. In either case, the pilot will keep their feet off the floor area where the brakes are and will rotate either to the side or down to apply the brakes. This is different than a traditional toe brake configuration in which the pilot will typically keep their heels on the floor, actuate the rudders, and when needed, rotate their feet forward and up onto the toe brakes to actuate them. Heel brakes are not necessarily any more difficult, but they just require a slightly different motion that pilots will have to become accustomed to when transitioning to a tailwheel aircraft with this type of brake installed.

Toe-brake-equipped tailwheel aircraft will be flown much like any other toe-brake-equipped aircraft, with pilots resting their feet on the floor, trying to keep their toes off the brakes until they need them, and then rotating their feet forward and onto the toe brakes.

When using either toe brakes or heel brakes, the tailwheel pilot must be more careful to apply the brakes evenly and only when needed. Applying brakes unevenly, applying only one brake, or applying the brakes when travelling too fast commonly results in added side load that can result in a ground loop. As I mentioned before, sparingly applying brakes is a tenet of tailwheel flying.

Braking effectiveness can also be different depending on the aircraft's particular manufacturer style of brakes. Most aircraft will have a modern, disk-style brake, but all aircraft will not necessarily have the same style of brakes. Older aircraft that have not received braking system upgrades may have less effective brake systems, and if so, it is better to know this ahead of time than figure it out during a first landing on a short field.

If the aircraft happens to not have brakes at all, obviously the pilot will need to consider this for any landing. The reality is that in many cases, and especially when operating on a grass runway, brakes are largely not needed for smaller tailwheel aircraft when a sufficiently long runway is present. Friction from the rolling tires will bring the aircraft to a stop within a reasonable distance. However, I am not saying that brakes aren't a nice thing to have, or that if your aircraft has them and they are broken you shouldn't have them fixed, but if you happen to fly an aircraft that is not equipped with brakes, planning to ensure that you use an adequately long runway is still perfectly acceptable.

Tandem or Side-by-Side Seating

Most tricycle-gear, general aviation aircraft have side-by-side seating. A few very common tailwheel aircraft break from this typical pattern and instead have a tandem seating configuration (with one person in front of the other). A few of the most common aircraft with tandem seating include Piper Cubs, Aeronca Champs, and Citabrias. Most of these makes and models are flown solo from the front seat, but some of the earlier Piper Cubs are flown from the rear seat when flown without a passenger. Usually containing two seats, the tandem seating configuration is seen in many common tailwheel aircraft that can be good for initial training and great general aviation flying planes for the average pilot. For many tailwheel pilots, flying from the center of the aircraft allows them to more easily "feel" if the aircraft is being dislodged from the centerline track during takeoff and landing, compared with flying a tailwheel aircraft with a side-by-side seating configuration.

In larger tailwheel aircraft, side-by-side seating is more common—typically aircraft with more than two seats will have a side-by-side seating configuration. Common general aviation examples of these include the Cessna 170 and 180, Stinson, and Maule aircraft. Flying these aircraft requires the pilot to look a little off-center when flying and tracking down the centerline.

Tailwheel pilots deciding between a side-by-side configuration and a tandem configuration should consider a few key differences and factors. How many seats does the pilot want in the aircraft? In some tandem seating aircraft, entry to the front or back seat may be easier or harder depending on where the wheel or wing struts fall in the entry door. Mobility of the pilot may be a factor in choosing which aircraft will be best. Size of the cabin can be a factor when considering between tandem or side-by-side seating. A Luscombe, Taylorcraft, or Cessna 120 or 140 tailwheel side-by-side aircraft offers less shoulder room per occupant, who have to sit next to each other, than an aircraft such as a Champ, in which the occupants sit front to back in two different seats. If you are a bigger pilot or your passengers are larger, the tandem seating may be more comfortable.

Engines

Engines can vary widely depending on the type of tailwheel aircraft. This brings up a variety of considerations that a pilot must think about.

Older, smaller aircraft are typically equipped with smaller, carbureted engines. These engines are more likely (some more than others) to encounter carburetor icing. In a number of carbureted engines, procedures have been established that require a pilot to use carburetor heat at all times—for example, when operating under 2,000 RPM on some engines. A great deal of information about carburetor icing is available for pilots to study, but following are three sources I recommend as especially helpful for review.

- AOPA Safety Brief, *Combating Carb Ice*
- FAA Special Airworthiness Information Bulletin, *Carburetor Icing Prevention*
- NTSB Safety Alert, *Engine Power Loss Due to Carburetor Icing*

(Find links to these and other resources on this book's Reader Resources webpage: www.asa2fly.com/reader/taildrag)

Take the time to consider the dangers of any engine specifics that may differ from those on other aircraft you have flown. A carbureted engine will have some different characteristics than a fuel-injected one.

Beyond carbureted or fuel-injected considerations, it's important to consider the effects of engine size—an aircraft with a larger engine will perform differently than one with a small engine. Overpowered airframes will have greater left-turning tendencies than the same airframes with smaller engines, but smaller engines will result in longer takeoff rolls and less climb ability to clear obstacles.

For many older aircraft, a wide variety of engine combinations may have been factory-installed or subsequently approved for installation. When examining and learning the characteristics of different engines, a little homework and discussion with experienced pilots and instructors can greatly enhance the safety of your operations.

•••

While the above sections cover a few of the important differences between the wide variety of tailwheel aircraft that a pilot may consider, there are no doubt many more, ranging from simple considerations such as how high you sit in the seat, to more noticeable differences such as whether it is a high-wing or low-wing aircraft. If you are transitioning between tailwheel aircraft, take the time to consider how the differences between the aircraft you have experience flying and the one you are aiming to fly will affect how the aircraft will handle and perform.

Chapter 13

Older Planes

Many available tailwheel aircraft are older. Although it's true that you can buy newly produced tailwheel aircraft such as Cubs, Citabrias, Huskies, and many aerobatic planes, the fact is that the bulk of the tailwheel aircraft on the market for rental or purchase are older aircraft, from an era when they were the standard for aircraft being produced by manufacturers. Flying older aircraft comes with opportunities, challenges, and in my opinion, some level of custodianship as a pilot.

Before the industry transitioned to making most general aviation aircraft with a tricycle-gear configuration, the predominant aircraft were ones such as Cessna 170s and Cessna 180s, Cubs, Champs, Stinsons, Luscombes, and Taylorcraft, to name only a few. From the 1930s through the 1960s, most of the aircraft produced for light general aviation consumers were tailwheel-equipped, and many of these aircraft are still flying today.

In many cases, these older aircraft offer unique opportunities for general aviation pilots to purchase airplanes that are still capable of being great personal and family aircraft. Frequently, good deals can be found on older aircraft that are in less demand and, as a result, this can allow a pilot to purchase them at significant savings compared to similar, slightly newer, tricycle-gear aircraft of the same size.

However, not all tailwheel aircraft are cheaper, as Cessna 170, Cessna 180, Cessna 190/195, and Piper Super Cub aircraft many times hold higher values as sought-after makes and models, but for aircraft such as Luscombes, Taylorcraft, and Stinsons, the prices are often a steal compared to other tricycle-gear aircraft with similar capabilities. A good friend of mine managed to sell his Cessna 150, buy a superbly restored Stinson 108-2, and even have some money left over afterward.

Older aircraft do have some challenges that are important for an owner to consider, including the availability of parts, mechanics, and manuals and documentation, as well as insurance premiums

Parts Availability

The older an aircraft is, the harder it can become to get parts. This is a common problem with many older tailwheel aircraft. In some cases, this may mean that when a part breaks, it will require making modifications and upgrades to the plane, replacing older parts with new compatible substitutes, or fabricating replacement parts completely from scratch (sometimes the most difficult and expensive option).

A pilot or owner of an older tailwheel aircraft will sometimes need to become good at salvaging or scrounging to keep the aircraft properly maintained.

Mechanic Availability

As many of the tailwheel aircraft that we fly get older, so do the mechanics that were familiar with them. In fact, many of these mechanics have retired or passed away well ahead of the retirement of the aircraft themselves. This can make finding an experienced and qualified mechanic somewhat difficult. The good news is that many of the older tailwheel aircraft are actually quite simply built, so a good mechanic who is not necessarily familiar with the particular make and model may be able to quickly learn the intricacies of some of the older aircraft.

Owners of older tailwheel aircraft many times find that they must become very familiar with their own aircraft and sometimes serve as the resource for the mechanic working on their equipment. By learning about some of the particular older aircraft, becoming a member of type clubs, or seeking out specific mechanics who are familiar with the makes and models they are flying, owners can increase the reliability of the mechanical services and their ability to keep these older aircraft serviceable.

If you are a pilot or owner of an older tailwheel aircraft, it's worth noting that there are FAA-approved preventative maintenance items that you should really consider learning to do on your own.

In 14 CFR Part 43 Appendix A (c) (www.ecfr.gov), the FAA lists all the things that pilots can do on their own aircraft. It includes work such as changing tires, servicing elastic shock absorber cords on landing gear, replacing bulbs (for items like landing or navigation lights), replacing or cleaning spark plugs, or changing the oil, which are just a few of the common things from the list that pilots often choose to do on their own.

Preventative maintenance is something that mechanically savvy or properly trained pilots can easily do on their own, and it can allow them to keep their aircraft operating when a mechanic is not available for basic items. Obviously, I cannot recommend going beyond this list without training and proper certification, but if you have a desire to do so, you would not be the first pilot in history to become airframe and powerplant (A&P) or even inspection authorization (IA) certificated as a result of starting to work on your own aircraft and developing a desire to learn more!

Insurance

The cost of insurance on a tailwheel aircraft will typically come at a premium compared to insurance for a similarly sized and valued tricycle-gear aircraft. This is especially true for pilots with little or no tailwheel flying experience. However, a good insurance agent will work with you, and if you are a little savvy you will understand that insurance coverage is somewhat of a negotiation. If a proposition of numbers of hours of flight experience or instruction is given, it may be countered with a minimum number of landings to be conducted for insurance coverage. The same could be considered for currency requirements.

As a pilot gets more experience either in a particular make and model or in tailwheel aircraft generally, the insurance premiums will abate to some degree. Note, however, that they will likely never be quite as low as in a similarly valued and sized tricycle-gear aircraft.

Manuals and Documentation Availability

Newer aircraft typically come with a thick pilot's operating handbook (POH) or airplane flight manual (AFM), extensive service manuals, or even training guides that have been developed by the manufacturers. These resources are typically missing or, at best, very thin for older aircraft.

A POH/AFM for a 1940's aircraft may consist of a few very select pages listing only the most basic information, such as recommended oil, a few basic speeds, and minimal systems descriptions. Many have little if any performance charts or data, and some do not even have weight and balance information. This leaves pilots fending for themselves in many respects. But do not despair just yet, as other resources are available. They just may not be the ones you are used to using.

For many older aircraft, previously mentioned type clubs are fantastic resources that pilots should seriously consider engaging with to gain more information. Frequently, a little internet searching can help a pilot ascertain good data for things such as V-speeds, performance data, and best flying practices. This should be supplemented by working with an instructor who is familiar with the make and model of the aircraft.

In some cases, information about aircraft almost falls into the realm of "lore." Learning to fly a Beach 18 or a DC-3 may mean spending some time with the crusty old guy who used to fly them when he first started flying in the old days, but who has probably forgotten more about flying than many of us will ever learn.

It may be that a seasoned pilot in a particular tailwheel aircraft inherently knows that with a crosswind greater than 5 knots, it is time to wheel land because the rudder loses too much effectiveness in the three-point stance—or any number of similar old-sage, pilot-wisdom types of knowledge that can be passed along. If you are going to be flying aircraft on which documentation is thin, scarce, or non-existent, spend the time to find someone who knows it well to supplement the knowledge base you won't be able to read about.

Benefits of Older Aircraft

Now that I have covered a few of the detractions of older aircraft, I really do have to highlight some of the opportunities these birds afford. Older tailwheel aircraft are great transition points for many pilots into other types of flying or into other equally rare and special birds.

For more than a few pilots, spending time learning to fly an Aeronca Champ with an old, local airport instructor has led into an opportunity to take a ride in that same instructor's T-6, which has subsequently led to flying more advanced warbird aircraft. Many historic warbird aircraft are tailwheel-equipped, and if you are a pilot who has no experience flying tailwheel aircraft, it is less likely that you will ever be given the reigns of something with more horsepower. World War II pilots were trained in aircraft such as Stearmans and Cubs before they moved on to more capable aircraft, and that same path is how many pilots of the modern generation also step their way onto flying more complex and high-performance historic aircraft.

The same holds true for pilots who may want to fly aerobatic, agricultural, or other working aircraft that are commonly tailwheel-equipped.

While these older tailwheel aircraft present some challenges, they also present many opportunities for pilots to gain new experience, become acquainted with new regimes of flight, and be a part of maintaining a historic legacy of some of our most cherished aircraft. In a sense, flying these older aircraft includes a level of stewardship as pilots. Many older aircraft are truly classics and can even be flying pieces of history.

My family owns a unique example of a tailwheel aircraft—a 1941 Meyers OTW biplane. From what we can tell, fewer than 20 of these planes are still flying, and even fewer still have their original Warner (radial) engine (from the 102 total that were ever built, according to my research). Having this aircraft in the family means we are now caretakers of one of the examples of the Meyers OTW. In essence, we are living history managers of this aircraft, and with the ownership and flying privileges of the aircraft comes a responsibility to the industry to keep it alive for another generation.

This privilege and responsibility is something that may come with many of the older tailwheel aircraft a pilot may fly or own.

Becoming involved with an older aircraft also can change your experience when you arrive at a new airport. People will come over and check out your plane as a unique example of our aviation history, not just another Cessna 172 production airplane (and I mean no offense, I still fly them, too) that looks identical to the last 15 that flew into the airport the same day.

Chapter 14

The Many Modifications of Tailwheel Aircraft

More than tricycle-gear aircraft, it seems that tailwheel aircraft often become the targets of modifications, upgrades, tweaks, adjustments, and general bastardization. Makes and models of tailwheel aircraft such as the Cessna 180/185, the Super Cub, and the Maule series of aircraft tend to have a wide variety of modifications made to them to improve their performance in short or rough field conditions. Commonly, these modifications are completed with supplemental type certificates (STCs) that have been approved to install or change equipment on the aircraft to accomplish goals of shorter takeoff, better performance, slower flight speeds, or a better ability to handle rough terrain.

Savvy tailwheel pilots will learn about modifications made to aircraft before flying them, even if they are just, "giving it a try." With that in mind, let's cover some of the common modifications that a pilot may find in tailwheel aircraft.

Bigger Engines

One of the most expensive and perhaps performance-enhancing modifications that can be made to a tailwheel aircraft is the installation of an engine larger than the size of the originally certificated engine in order to provide more horsepower. Bigger engines can increase weight-hauling capacities, decrease takeoff distances, or allow the aircraft to use larger propellers or constant-speed propellers that were not able to be used in the original design.

However, there are some potential disadvantages that go along with bigger engines. A heavier engine on the front of the aircraft can move the center of gravity forward, in some cases requiring that ballast be used in the aft sections of the aircraft when flying without rear passengers or cargo. Additionally, the bigger the engine, the more fuel it burns. Unless fuel capacity has been increased with larger fuel tanks on the aircraft, this can limit the aircraft's range because it will burn more gallons of fuel per hour. Specific engines may be a better or worse match for a particular airframe, so take the time to learn about the effects if an engine change was made on an aircraft you plan to fly.

Propeller Changes

Aircraft propellers sometimes are changed to achieve different performance enhancements, either in conjunction with an engine change or as a solitary upgrade. Some fixed-pitch propellers have better climb performance, others are optimized to have better cruise performance, and some are pitched to be somewhere in-between. Most aircraft are originally equipped with propellers that have performance somewhere in the middle.

Many tailwheel aircraft have been modified with propellers that pick a specific performance target. More commonly, the target is focused on climb performance by using a propeller that is pitched to give the best climb performance. This will improve short-field takeoff performance but will sacrifice cruise speed.

In other cases, aircraft are modified by the installation of a constant-speed propeller even though they were originally equipped with fixed-pitch propeller systems. In these cases, the constant-speed propeller system is typically a little heavier, which may bring the center of gravity slightly forward, and it allows the pilot to select the pitch for best performance in various phases of flight.

A change in the number of blades is another modification that can be found on many tailwheel aircraft. To achieve added efficiency, some propellers are upgraded from two- to three-blade configurations. The three-blade configuration can result in shorter propeller lengths, which provides greater ground clearance, quieter propeller noise, and in some cases better climb or cruise performance.

Short-Field Performance Modifications

The most common modifications made to many tailwheel aircraft are intended to enhance short-field performance. The purpose of these is to allow the aircraft to accelerate to takeoff speed faster, to increase the efficiency of the airflow over the wing, or to decrease the stall speed to allow the aircraft to lift off the ground at a lower-than-original airspeed.

Vortex generators (VGs) are frequently installed on the upper surface of the wings to channel the airflow over the top of the wings more efficiently. The added efficiency of airflow over the wing will commonly decrease both the aircraft's stall speeds and the distance required to lift off the ground. Another benefit of VGs is usually an allowable increase in gross weight for the aircraft, allowing the pilot to carry more cargo. VGs are little fins placed just behind the leading edge of the upper surface of the wing in a specific pattern. It is worth noting that if a small number of these are missing (they can easily be broken off by a line service attendant dragging a fuel hose across the wing or by someone washing the plane accidentally scrubbing them off), it will nullify the allowable benefits that an STC for VGs provides.

"Drooping" wing tips or winglets are also methods of modifying an aircraft to affect the airflow over the wing, enhancing performance by changing the airflow as it spills out the end of the wing. The effects of these are similar to those of VGs, and in many cases a pilot will find VGs combined with winglets or drooping wing tips on some makes and models of aircraft to even further increase short-field performance.

Big Tires

Monster trucks have big tires so they can drive over other things. Doing this in an aircraft probably is not a very good idea, but it doesn't mean that having bigger tires is never useful. For tailwheel aircraft, bigger tires are commonly used when flying on rough or unimproved runways or even in places that are not actual runways but still can serve as landing places for aircraft.

Planes that commonly use paved runways or good grass runways will typically have smaller tires, comparable to those on the average

Cessna 172 or Piper Warrior. When aircraft owners want to fly and land their aircraft on rougher runways, they many times increase the size of their aircraft's tires and lower the tire pressure. This allows the aircraft to "roll over" bumps or rough runway areas more easily without bouncing, as might occur if using smaller and harder tires. When it comes to tire options, there is a middle ground where an aircraft can be equipped with treaded tires that are bigger and that can still be operated at only slightly lower pressures. This is more common than the extreme "bush" wheels that are big, non-treaded, balloon-style tires with low pressure.

Bush wheels in the extreme are intended to be landed off of paved runways the majority of the time. They are serviced with lower air pressure and are soft when contacting the ground on landing. These are well-suited to better accommodate landing on rough surfaces. With a little searching on the Internet, you can find some fantastic videos of talented pilots taking aircraft equipped with these bush wheels (and other modifications) in gravel bars on rivers, in short backcountry air strips, or even flying off the edges of mountainsides. I can't recommend that you attempt any of these, but I can tell you that some of the modifications made to tailwheel aircraft have allowed highly talented (and sometimes very lucky) pilots to accomplish these feats.

So why don't we see all aircraft equipped with big, non-treaded bush wheels? Well, with the benefits of being suited to rough surface runways come some detriments. Bush wheels are more likely to hydroplane on a paved runway; their softer pressure allows them to "squish" down onto the runway more during a landing, which can make them feel stickier and make it harder to correct side-to-side displacement of the aircraft; and without tread, the tires are much more quickly degraded by repeated operations on pavement. Larger tires can also increase drag. They are fun to fly in the correct environment, but can get expensive to replace if you eat them up on paved runways too quickly.

In general, smaller tires with higher pressure will be more likely to bounce but will be better suited to paved runway operations. Bigger, softer tires will be less likely to bounce, be more likely to feel "grabby" on paved runways, and be easily damaged by repeated operations on paved runways.

Somewhat obviously, changing tire sizes may mean that if your aircraft was originally equipped with wheel pants, they may no longer fit to be installed. Although not usually even considered for a beginning tailwheel pilot, it is not acceptable to just reduce tire pressure to get a softer landing, because as a tire squats more during a landing, the clearance between the tire and the brake may be compromised. Before making any change in tire configurations, all of these factors should be carefully considered, as well as other system modifications that may be required to accommodate any tire size changes.

Main Gear Modifications

Modifications to the main gear system can be very valuable in some aircraft, although they are not as common as other alterations. Modifications can be made to the main gear on particular models of aircraft to make landings less bouncy or to make the gear more forgiving or better able to handle rough surfaces. Springs, bungees, or other parts can be changed to make the aircraft perform differently on the main gear.

One of the most commonly discussed gear modifications in the tailwheel community is the P. Ponk gear modification for the Cessna 170/180/185/L19 series of aircraft. It is intended to reduce the possibility of landing gear failure during a ground loop or gear strike and to minimize the damage that could result from these events. This modification is commonly considered to make the aircraft perform a little better during the landings.

In some aircraft, changes to the main gear configuration can make the landing characteristics more docile and be well worth the investment for an owner.

Bungees vs. Spring Steel Gear

The two major types of main landing gear found in tailwheel aircraft are bungee and spring steel systems.

The more modern, spring steel landing gear systems are mechanically simple, allowing the metal gear itself to flex during the landing process while being lightweight and requiring very little maintenance. Conversely, bungee cord systems are more likely to need maintenance, and they are literally comprised of a series of elastic bungee cords that during landing transfer the impact load to the aircraft with some shock absorption to help minimize bouncing by dissipating energy from the touchdown.

Many tailwheel pilots will tell you that the spring steel gear systems are more "bouncy," resulting in more bounces during landing than the more forgiving bungee systems. While both systems can certainly absorb some shock during a landing (definitely more than historically equipped aircraft that had fixed gear with no shock absorption), if enough downward force is experienced on any landing, the result will be a bounce—or worse.

It is usually considered easier to transition from tailwheels equipped with spring steel gear to aircraft equipped with bungee gear than vice versa. Fly them both and make the decision for yourself!

Tail Wheel Changes

Changes in the tailwheel mechanisms on aircraft are becoming more frequently seen. In some cases, this is the result of a lack of available replacement parts for the systems on older aircraft, which often means that to fix any damage or maintenance issues, the pilot is forced to upgrade to newer systems or pieces of equipment.

Tail wheels are frequently upgraded to larger sizes to better accommodate grass or unimproved runway operations. A bigger tail wheel will be less likely to vibrate or bounce on rougher surfaces than a smaller, harder tailwheel.

Aircraft that originally had skids or free-castering tail wheels are in many cases upgraded to locking or steerable tail wheels to improve their ground handling characteristics. In many cases, these upgrades are downright affordable compared to many other aircraft parts or modifications that can be relatively expensive.

•••

All of these and other potential modifications mean that during their flying careers, tailwheel pilots may fly multiple aircraft of the same make and model that could have very different handling characteristics. As an example, so far in my flying, I have flown Cessna 170 aircraft with regular tires, bigger treaded tires, and smooth bush wheels; with fixed cruise propellers, fixed climb propellers, and constant-speed propellers; with and without the P. Ponk gear modification; with VGs and without; with droop-tip wings and straight wings; with a steerable tail wheel and a free-castering tail wheel; and with three different engine sizes ranging from 145 hp to 210 hp. Imagine all of these combinations and how many different variations of them you could come up with on one single make and model of aircraft.

With all aircraft modifications, it is critical that a pilot obtain and become familiar with any supplemental data that is published that changes the original pilot's operating handbook or airplane flight manual. Critical data for weight and balance, takeoff and landing distances, and operating limitations such as V-speeds or RPM speed ranges can all be different than those originally published for the aircraft. These are important updates to make to a pilot's operating checklists and practices for any modified aircraft.

Chapter 15

Primary Training and Testing in a Tailwheel Aircraft

As an examiner who is also a tailwheel instructor with experience in a variety of tailwheel aircraft, I do on occasion conduct practical tests in tailwheel aircraft. It is by far not as common as it may have been in the past, but it does still happen, and there are fewer and fewer examiners available who are tailwheel qualified, current, and—more importantly—proficient.

Pilots who originally train in a tailwheel aircraft many times wonder what the big deal is for pilots who transition after learning to fly in a different type of aircraft. This is a great example of the primacy of training. If you learn in a tailwheel initially, it will become second nature to fly a tailwheel. If a pilot's long-term goal is to fly a tailwheel, it can be worth seeking out initial training in a tailwheel aircraft. The same concerns hold true—and are in fact even more important—for instructors interested in providing instruction in tailwheel aircraft, and for students when choosing their own instructor. It becomes more critical to have an experienced and proficient instructor for a primary student who does not already have any piloting experience to rely upon.

When it comes time for your test, picking the correct examiner will also be important. While the examiner does not fly on the day of the practical test, make sure the examiner is familiar with the aircraft and is tailwheel proficient (they are required to be tailwheel endorsed to conduct the test) to ensure a proper test will be administered. If the examiner is not familiar with your aircraft, they are not going to be properly able to give you a test.

Although there can be additional logistical challenges in setting up initial pilot training in a tailwheel aircraft, it is well worth finding solutions to these challenges if a pilot's end goal is to fly primarily tailwheel aircraft once certificated.

This is especially valuable for pilots who may be seeking a career in agricultural flight operations, who want to fly for a hobby or professionally in aerobatic aircraft, or who believe they will be looking to use aircraft for backcountry or unimproved airport flying after completing training. Consider what type of flying you plan to do in the future before determining if learning in a tailwheel aircraft is the best fit. If that turns out to be the case, it may be better to initially learn to fly in a tailwheel aircraft and gain broader experience rather than just complete a transition after initial pilot training.

Chapter 16

So You Want To Be a Tailwheel Instructor

Becoming a tailwheel instructor is one of the most rewarding things I have done as a pilot, instructor, and examiner. It has allowed me to fly aircraft that are unique, special, historic, and generally pretty darn fun. I have flown tailwheel aircraft into strips (and non-runways) to which I would have never flown a tricycle-gear aircraft. And, to be honest, I just think they look cooler. But it hasn't been all flowers and candy.

When I talk with instructors who want to begin instructing in tailwheel aircraft, the first thing I tell them is that if they are going to do it, they should be willing to have an accident or incident on their pilot record.

You may ask, "What? Really?"

I admit that it is not a sure thing, and many tailwheel instructors have not had to deal with an accident or incident, but it is statistically more likely to occur for tailwheel instructors than for instructors who operate only in tricycle-gear aircraft. This is a bit harsh, but it is a great point to start a conversation about instructing in tailwheel aircraft. When done correctly, safely, and proficiently, tailwheel instruction doesn't always have to result in this, but instructors in tailwheel aircraft are simply more likely than those in tricycle-gear aircraft to encounter a student blunder that is unrecoverable by the instructor.

Full disclosure here: it has happened to me twice. One occasion was in a Cessna 170 where we were a little left of runway centerline on touchdown and I asked the student (a private pilot training student) to apply "a little right rudder" to bring us back to the centerline. He was wearing larger work boots that day, and when he went to apply right rudder, his boots stuck and he fully applied that right rudder. This caused a momentary change in momentum, the tail of the aircraft started to go around to our left, and we experienced an approximate 70-degree ground loop, leaving us off the runway on the right side. The momentum caused the left wing to dip and strike the ground, and the end result was some required maintenance to the aircraft.

The second occurrence was in a Maule M5 that the transitioning pilot (who had purchased the aircraft) over-rotated just above touchdown, causing the tail wheel to contact the ground rather firmly. To this day, I am not sure if the impact was actually enough to cause the problem, or if the tail spring had been previously damaged, but the tail spring broke, leaving us dragging our tail and pulling the tail wheel behind with minimal directional control as we "rolled out" the landing.

On numerous occasions and in multiple different aircraft, I have experienced a tail spring falling off, causing the tail wheel to pull to one side or the other during takeoff or landing. So far, I have been able to mitigate these events, but I will not tell you that will always be possible. A tail spring can easily become dislodged or loosened when operating off of rougher sod or grass runways, and this can be the factor leading to a difficult or dangerous takeoff or landing.

A tailwheel instructor must be on top of their game for these types of events and do their best to manage these incidents if they occur. Instructors flying in tricycle-gear aircraft many times will relax a little and give more leeway to students as they become generally proficient in their landings. But tailwheel instructors must stay vigilant and avoid doing this, as it will increase the time it takes them to respond, and when less time is available, it can limit their ability to respond to a student error fast enough to correct it.

Generally, a tailwheel instructor needs to be sure to actively monitor the student during takeoff and landing and be prepared to step in with direction or assistance. Instructors must not only remain proficient, but before providing any instruction, it is a smart idea for them to ensure they are proficient in the particular make and model of aircraft being flown.

When I have clients who ask me to instruct in a make and model of tailwheel aircraft I have not flown for a period of time, I will typically ask to "borrow" the aircraft for a couple of flights on my own to get re-acquainted with the aircraft before I attempt any initial or transition instruction for the customer. If it is a plane I have never flown, I either find the client another instructor who is proficient, or find an instructor who can help me become proficient before I try to work with the client.

I have learned some of these lessons the hard way, but have known other pilots who have taken longer or learned them with more repercussions. Take these words seriously if you are an instructor who is considering becoming a tailwheel instructor part- or full-time. There is nothing wrong with telling a customer that you are not the correct instructor for their particular needs.

With this in mind, the question becomes, how do you get started as a tailwheel instructor? The short answer is by first gaining a bunch of experience in tailwheel aircraft.

Most instructors begin by getting a tailwheel endorsement of their own and then doing anything they can to increase their experience. Some good ways to accomplish this are to find other tailwheel pilots who will let you fly with them, conduct flight reviews in tailwheel aircraft, and provide instrument proficiency checks (IPCs) to fellow pilots. Every bit of experience you can get in a tailwheel will help build the total time you need to eventually make an insurance underwriter approve you to fly and instruct in tailwheel aircraft.

A few less common but great ways to gain tailwheel experience are to volunteer (or if possible, get paid) to be a tow pilot for gliders (many glider tow aircraft are tailwheel-equipped) or buy a plane to get the experience. While it may seem like buying a plane is out of reach for many people, there are many very reasonably priced, classic aircraft that are tailwheel. With an eye to the long game, you could buy a tailwheel and use it to gain experience and then later use it as a rental aircraft in which you could provide instruction, turning it into a future profit center.

There is no quick, easy way to get the experience you will need, so take the time to do it right. Get more instruction along the way, and if you are transitioning into a new aircraft, find another instructor or experienced pilot familiar with the particular make and model to fly with you for the first couple of flights.

Chapter 17

"General Rules" of Tailwheel Flying

Every instructor or tailwheel pilot you encounter will have some "sage advice" to offer you that they claim will keep you from wrecking your plane or killing yourself. No one thing will do that, but for discussion purposes, and to some degree entertainment, I will share a few of the "rules" of tailwheel flying that commonly get spread around in our aviation community.

In addition to all of the points already covered in this book, following are additional tips to contemplate that will be helpful during your own tailwheel flying.

Busy feet are happy feet. Keep busy, but don't overcorrect.
Many tailwheel instructors will tell you that if you stop moving your feet, you have stopped flying the plane. Think about dancing: if you stop moving your feet while on the dance floor with your significant other, you have stopped dancing with them. This doesn't mean you always have to be moving a lot, but if you are not moving your feet during takeoff and landings, then you are not correcting for any potential side drift. You can stop using your feet when flying a tailwheel aircraft when you get out.

Keep the tail behind the airplane.
This one should be obvious, but sometimes the obvious can be a good reminder.

Sit as high as possible.
This allows you the best possible view over the cowl of the aircraft and will help in taxi, takeoff, and landing operations. As long as you can still reach the rudders and are in a comfortable position, sitting a bit higher to increase visibility is valuable, as it will always make it easier for you to see what is happening during your takeoff or landing.

Stay off the brakes until they are absolutely necessary for stopping.
Brakes applied in an uncoordinated fashion can easily lead to a ground loop. Therefore, do not use them until the aircraft has slowed down, and then be sure to stay as coordinated as possible.

Know what a three-point position looks like in the plane.
Find a spot on the cowl or side to determine a good view angle for a three-point stance. Use the taxi out to learn the position of the nose angle. The way you taxi is the way you land (three-point stance). Also, taxi attitude = go-around pitch.

Adding power slowly during a takeoff (a three-second count) works well for most aircraft.
This will keep you from experiencing too much torque, accelerating too quickly, or inciting the likelihood of a ground loop.

Dutch rolls are good rudder practice.
A less commonly taught maneuver nowadays, Dutch rolls can actually be a good training exercise to do when practicing in tailwheel aircraft where keeping the aircraft aligned with the long line of the runway becomes more critical. Essentially, a Dutch roll is when the airplane is flown with a combination of "tail-wagging" and rocking from side to side. When completing a Dutch roll, think of a beam of light at the end of the runway. It probably goes without saying, but these are obviously best to be practiced at altitude, not during a landing.

Remember: speed vs. altitude (pitch for airspeed, power for altitude).

If you are low on approach, pulling back will cause you to slow down and stall. Push forward if you need to gain airspeed, add power if you need to gain altitude, or do both if you need to gain both. If you don't have enough room to do either, go around and try again.

Tailwheel airplanes have rudder steering and tailwheel steering (assuming it is not a free-castering tailwheel aircraft).

You should have one before you give up the other. Rudder steering is used while there is sufficient airflow to steer the aircraft with the rudder. Tailwheel steering works when the wheel is on the ground and the tailwheel springs can affect steering.

Tailwheel aircraft with narrow gears and high centers of gravity are more susceptible to ground loops.

Be aware of how your aircraft is configured, and review this book's section discussing ground loops.

The size of the vertical fin on the aircraft determines the aircraft's weathervaning tendencies.

The bigger the tail vertical fin, the more it will be affected by wind, especially in a crosswind. If your aircraft has a very large vertical fin—and in a worst case, a small rudder—your ability to counteract any sideways displacement of the tail will be limited.

Bounces = Go Arounds!

This does not mean you can never recover from a bounce, but in most cases it is safer to go around and try the landing again.

Resources

Visit the Reader Resources page for this title to access these and other resources: www.asa2fly.com/reader/taildrag

The material covered in this book should not be the only resource considered by aspiring tailwheel pilots or those looking to expand their skills. While there are many websites that provide varying degrees of content depth, the following resources are a few that I use with my own students and that I have found to be reliable and helpful. I am hopeful that you will also find them useful.

Damian DelGaizo's *Tailwheel: 101* **and** *Tailwheel: 201—Beyond the Basics*

This is a great video series if you want to dive deeper into tailwheel training, including both *Tailwheel: 101* and *Tailwheel: 201* for those who want to learn more. The video is available in both digital and DVD formats.

▸ tailwheel101.com

Conventional Gear: Flying a Taildragger
By David Robson

David Robson's book, published by Aviation Supplies & Academics (ASA), describes the general tailwheel flying process and actions and also includes more detailed discussion of some commonly recognized tailwheel aircraft. These include popular aircraft such as the Cessna 185 and Citabria, as well as some less common but visible aircraft such as the DC3 and the Tiger Moth.

▸ www.asa2fly.com

Notes on the Tailwheel Checkout and an Introduction to Ski Flying
By Burke Mees
Published by ASA, Burke Mees's book explains the general tailwheel flying process but also goes into specific discussion about ski flying, which is most commonly accomplished in aircraft that are tailwheel-equipped.

▸ www.asa2fly.com

The Compleat Taildragger Pilot
By Harvey S. Plourde
This book was originally published in 1991 but remains a great resource for pilots when attempting to learn more about tailwheel flying or transitioning. It details in depth the fundamentals of aerodynamics related to tailwheel aircraft. This book is one I consider almost required reading for my own tailwheel students.

Stick and Rudder: An Explanation of the Art of Flying
By Wolfgang Langewiesche
This is a classic book that should be on the reading list of all good taildragger pilots. While the book does not specifically focus on just tailwheel flying, much of the content is written from the perspective of a taildragger pilot. Originally published in 1944 and updated in 1972, the fundamentals in the book remain ever pertinent to modern tailwheel flying.

Taming the Taildragger: A Flight Manual for Classic Tailwheel Aircraft
By John Ball
A well-written book on tailwheel flying that focuses more on older types of tailwheel aircraft. It is one of the few books that details such things as preheating smaller engines, hand propping procedures, and flying aircraft without electrical systems. I am not sure if it is in current print anymore, but many used copies can be found. Originally published in 1977 and updated in 1987, its content still holds value, especially in regards to flying older aircraft of the era.

"Flying the Tailwheel: The Checkout"
By Rick Durden, published on AVweb
This is a helpful article that discusses the tailwheel checkout process and some additional tips on tailwheel flying.

▸ www.avweb.com/news/features/Flying-Tailwheel-The-Checkout-225192-1.html

"Tailwheel Pilot: What's a Ground Loop?"
By Thomas P. Turner, published by AVEMCO
A good article describing a ground loop in detail; worth the read.

▸ www.avemco.com/information/blogs/tailwheel-training.aspx

Tailwheel Airplanes Study Material
Material provided by Tailwheels Etc. based in Lakeland, Florida, this particular webpage is used by their instructors when introducing students to transitioning to tailwheel flying. If you like their material, you would definitely like their instruction also.

▸ www.tailwheelsetc.com/tailwheel_study_material.html

The Tailwheel Endorsement

A pilot who did not log tailwheel aircraft time prior to April 15, 1991, is required to have an endorsement. While the FAA does not establish a minimum numerical amount of flight time that must be completed to accomplish this endorsement with an instructor, 14 CFR §61.31(i) does detail that the following must be accomplished:

(1) Except as provided in paragraph (i)(2) of this section, no person may act as pilot in command of a tailwheel airplane unless that person has received and logged flight training from an authorized instructor in a tailwheel airplane and received an endorsement in the person's logbook from an authorized instructor who found the person proficient in the operation of a tailwheel airplane. The flight training must include at least the following maneuvers and procedures:

    (i) Normal and crosswind takeoffs and landings;

    (ii) Wheel landings (unless the manufacturer has recommended against such landings); and

    (iii) Go-around procedures.

(2) The training and endorsement required by paragraph (i)(1) of this section is not required if the person logged pilot-in-command time in a tailwheel airplane before April 15, 1991.

When this is completed, the instructor can use the following endorsement language to sign-off the student (this language can be found in the current FAA Advisory Circular 61-65):

> To act as pilot in command in a tailwheel airplane: §61.31(i).
> I certify that [First name, MI, Last name], [grade of pilot certificate], [certificate number], has received the required training of § 61.31(i) in a [make and model of tailwheel airplane]. I have determined that [he/she] is proficient in the operation of a tailwheel airplane.
> /s/ [date] J. J. Jones 987654321CFI Exp. 12-31-19

Of note, this endorsement is not required for a pilot who is initially training in a tailwheel aircraft for their pilot certificate. In that case, a solo endorsement in the particular make and model is sufficient—with a caveat: once the pilot obtains their pilot certificate through completion of a practical test, the solo endorsement becomes no longer valid and the pilot is then required to have the tailwheel endorsement. So, for an instructor and student who are conducting primary training in a tailwheel aircraft, it is advised that in addition to a make and model solo endorsement, a tailwheel endorsement also be completed prior to the completion of the practical test. As an examiner, I have on a few occasions found myself in a situation in which an applicant flew to a practical test on their solo privileges, passed the test, and then in absence of a tailwheel endorsement, was initially unauthorized to fly themselves home. I then completed a second flight with them to issue a tailwheel endorsement (it cannot be issued based on the conduct of the practical test, since a practical test is not considered giving of instruction).

About the Author

Jason Blair is an active instructor and FAA-designated pilot examiner who has worked for many years in the aviation training industry. He has flown and instructed in more than 90 makes and models of general aviation aircraft, many of them tailwheel, and through his experience has learned enough to share some knowledge that may be useful to others. He writes for multiple aviation publications and has worked for and with aviation associations and the FAA as an industry representative within the general aviation community.

To learn more about Jason Blair and his industry involvement, visit www.JasonBlair.net.